SIR WINSTON CHURCHILL ON HIS 79TH BIRTHDAY

CHURCHILL

THE MAN OF THE CENTURY

A Pictorial Biography

Edited by NEIL FERRIER

MCMLV

LORD WARDEN AND ADMIRAL OF THE CINQUE PORTS, 1946

ILLUSTRIOUS ANCESTORS

Some families produce eminent men for generation after generation, but genius is usually solitary. Where it comes from no-one knows : it seldom perpetuates itself. The Nelsons, Napoleons and Cromwells blaze up from obscurity and with their deaths the strain carries on as though it had never bred such unlikely creatures. Winston Leonard Spencer Churchill, born on the thirtieth of November, 1874 came of a family that had already played a leading part twice in the nation's story and he has always been, rightly, very conscious of its glories. Many boys look to the future with the vaguest of aspirations, but to Winston the " glories of our blood and state " were from the first both a guiding light and the mark at which one aimed. He was born to the benevolent exercise of power, as practised by his father, and also to the knowledge that a man must be ready to lay down his life for what he holds dear or he will not long retain it. Soldiering was in his blood.

JOHN CHURCHILL, DUKE OF MARLBOROUGH, 1650–1722

The founder of the family's fortunes, had been one of the ablest generals in England's history. It was in appreciation for his great victory over the French and Bavarian armies at *Blenheim* that he was given, by Queen Anne and his country, the palace of that name—in which Winston was born. Winston's father, Lord Randolph Churchill, 1849-95 (right) had risen to a position of great power within the Conservative party in the ' eighties ' by his realisation of the need for " Tory democracy ", a socially-conscious policy likely to appeal to the great new electorate then being enfranchised. Later Winston was to write of his father with deep sympathy and understanding. Later also, he was in his early years as a politician to echo Lord Randolph's pleas for " retrenchment and reform ".

LORD RANDOLPH CHURCHILL, 1849–95

WINSTON WITH HIS MOTHER AND HIS YOUNGER BROTHER JOHN
BLENHEIM PALACE

THE SCHOOLBOY

One of the major influences in Winston's life has been the fact that mixed with his English blood is another strain deriving from his American mother, Jennie Jerome, daughter of the fabulous millionaire Leonard Jerome. Apart from its general bearing on his character, this connection with the New World was to stand him in good stead when American sympathy and help of the "lease-lend" variety were so urgently needed in the early years of the Second World War. Here Winston is seen (opposite) with his mother and brother, and here too is Blenheim Palace, a symbol of continuity in national affairs not lost on the boy who was later to say, " it is in adversity . . . that the character of our slowly-wrought institutions reveals its latent, invincible strength."

As a schoolboy Winston showed little promise of brilliance. Lord Randolph who had hoped to see him established at the bar was forced to change his mind and let him adopt an army career. At Harrow, however, Winston did give two clear signs of his potentialities by becoming the Public Schools Fencing Champion and by winning a prize for a faultless recitation of a large slice of the *Lays of Ancient Rome*. The picture below shows a view of the Old Schools at Harrow.

HARROW SCHOOL

ARMY CADET

10

THE YOUNG OFFICER

At Sandhurst the young Churchill was faced for the first time with information that seemed to him worth acquiring, information which could be applied in action. He worked hard and played hard with the result that in 1894 he passed out eighth in a batch of one hundred and fifty—and having acquired that love of horses that was later to enliven his leisure with the delights of polo and racing. The army practice of honouring with real devotion institutions and customs, which are with another part of the mind looked upon as mildly comical or even irrelevant, was very much in the Churchill pattern of preserving the past but altering one's attitude to it in the light of present needs. Later, visits to Harrow, the scene of his inauspicious start in life, were to demonstrate the same mixture of loyalty and humorous insight.

AT THE AGE OF TWENTY-ONE

SUBALTERN IN INDIA

In January 1895 Lord Randolph died. With him died Winston's hopes of aiding him to regain the great place from which he had been ousted. In March Winston joined the *4th Hussars* (above). During the next three years he saw garrison service in England and India but contrived to get a far wider experience of active service conditions than most of his contemporaries. First he took part as an observer in the Cuban War, then later in India he got himself attached to two fighting expeditions. It was about this time also that he laid the foundations of two of his future "careers"—as historian and journalist—with a book *The Malakand Field Force* and with articles for the *Daily Telegraph* designed to pay the cost of his unofficial "attachments". Finally he contrived to take part in Kitchener's Sudan expedition, including the last full-scale cavalry charge at Omdurman.

£25

(Twenty-five Pounds stg.) REWARD is offered by the Sub-Commission of the fifth division, on behalf of the Special Constable of the said division, to anyone who brings the escaped prisioner of war

CHURCHILL,

dead or alive to this office.

For the Sub-Commission of the fifth division,

(Signed) LODK. de HAAS, Sec.

DURBAN—1899

THE SOUTH AFRICAN WAR

Churchill now determined to go into politics and resigned his commission. In 1899 he stood for one of the two Conservative seats at Oldham but lost it by fifteen hundred votes. Almost immediately, however, the South African War broke out and he at once set off as the correspondent of the *Morning Post*. While in pursuit of a " scoop ", the armoured train in which he was riding was derailed by the Boers. Churchill—his non-combatant status forgotten—set about organising its defence but was captured. Treated leniently, under the circumstances, as a prisoner of war, he escaped dramatically and in spite of the £25 reward offered for his recapture made his way to Durban where he was feted as a hero and had to address the crowd.

FIRST STEPS IN POLITICS

As a man in the public eye he found no difficulty in getting elected at Oldham in 1900 and spoke strongly in Parliament on behalf of the defeated Boers. In 1904, following his father's doctrine of "retrenchment" in the Service Estimates and in support of Free Trade, Churchill became a Liberal. Elected for Manchester North West in December 1905, he was soon in Office, first under Sir Henry Campbell Bannerman and later under Herbert Asquith as, successively, Under-Secretary of State for the Colonies, President of the Board of Trade and, in 1910, Home Secretary. By the latter date he had lost his Manchester seat but had gained another in Dundee. These pictures show him in 1908, electioneering in Manchester and at No. 10 Downing Street.

MRS. CHURCHILL

In 1908 Churchill married Miss Clementine Ogilvie Hozier who was to aid him so much throughout his career by her methodical, disciplined yet unobtrusive ordering of his household, and by an inflexible power of " getting things done " second only to his own. At this time too began his interest in social amelioration, fostered by his friendship with David Lloyd George, also a growing realisation of the menace of Germany's armed might.

MR. AND MRS. CHURCHILL IN 1910

This picture of Churchill and Mrs. Churchill watching army manoeuvres at Aldershot in 1910 with General Bruce Hamilton is characteristic of two aspects of Churchill's make-up—the inability to be content with knowing only his own " fragment of the puzzle " in national or international affairs and his need (as much mental as physical) to " dress the part " he is living at any particular moment.

15

CHURCHILL WITH LLOYD GEORGE

In many ways Churchill looked to Lloyd George as his guide and mentor. Together they were to work for such causes as the founding of the first National Insurance scheme and the curtailing of the absolute veto of the House of Lords. At this time, 1910, Churchill had ceased his opposition to the expansion of the fleet, realising that the country's danger must outweigh any attachment to family principles. Thus the way was opening for the two men to work together later in England's hour of need.

SIDNEY STREET

A hint of the melodramatic streak in Churchill's nature was revealed by the Sidney Street affair (1911). On this occasion a gang of desperate criminals had been cornered in a house in Whitechapel and as Home Secretary he insisted on involving himself in the proceedings. The Home Secretary's place was obviously at his desk, to which would flow in due course official reports on the progress of the siege. To Churchill, however, inaction in the face of danger was unthinkable. Frowned on at the time, this exploit showed a trait later not unwelcome in bomb-scarred London. At the scene of the battle (below); giving evidence at the subsequent enquiry (right).

FIRST LORD OF THE ADMIRALTY

In 1911 Churchill became First Lord of the Admiralty, an office which he held until popular feeling turned against him after the failure of the Dardanelles Campaign in 1915. Whatever is thought of that costly failure, Churchill was responsible for none of the hesitations and delays that contributed to it so materially, whilst there is no doubt that with Lord Fisher he built up a Navy that saved England from invasion in 1914.

With one eye now constantly turned to Germany, Churchill made a point of finding his way there in 1913 to watch the German army manoeuvres. He is seen here (above opposite) with the Kaiser and (below opposite) with F. E. Smith later to be Lord Chancellor. At home Churchill was working to integrate the plans of the Army and the Navy for landing a force on the continent should it be necessary. Jellicoe, a comparatively junior officer, had been made Second in Command of the Home Fleet, the Navy had been given new speed by changing over from coal to oil and a new punch by the inclusion of 15 inch guns (a dangerous innovation, many thought) in its latest battleships.

WITH LORD FISHER IN 1913

WITH THE KAISER AT GERMAN ARMY MANOEUVRES IN 1913

SEATED WITH F. E. SMITH, AFTERWARDS LORD BIRKENHEAD, AT ARMY MANOEUVRES

One of Churchill's most characteristic traits has always been his ability to see the importance—even the need—of "the new thing". In the Second World War there was the Mulberry Harbour, largely the outcome of one of his suggestions. But right through his career there has been this readiness to get away from the conventional approach to a problem, as in his advocacy in both wars of the "soft underbelly" approach through eastern Europe. From the first days of flying he realised the significance of the aeroplane both as a weapon of war and a strengthener of peaceful ties. An early pilot, he remained undismayed by a number of crashes and took a most active interest in the expansion of the Air Force. Later his support for the newly-invented Radar during the period when he was out of office—but on the Committee of Imperial Defence for Air Defence Research— enabled the "Few" of the battle of Britain to defeat the might of Germany's Luftwaffe,

TOP, VISITING THE CENTRAL FLYING SCHOOL, SEPTEMBER, 1912

CENTRE, A FLIGHT OVER PORTSMOUTH HARBOUR, 1914

BOTTOM, ON A TRANSATLANTIC FLIGHT TO THE BERMUDA CONFERENCE, 1942

WEAPONS

and his own startling mobility in that war owed much to the weapon he had helped to forge. Yet with the tank, the other great factor in the modern "war of mobility" he had an even more intimate connection. It was during his tenure of the Admiralty in the First World War that his mind turned to the problem of how to circumvent the stalemate of trench warfare on the Western Front. There, defence, based on the machine-gun, the mortar and heavy artillery, rendered attack hideously wasteful and almost useless.—But if something immune to bullets and capable of straddling trenches could be evolved?—From this germ came the "landships", experimented with during his Admiralty days. And from the landship came the tank that, largely wasted in the First World War, later came into its own in the Western Desert at the grave risk—deliberately undertaken by Churchill—of leaving England almost defenceless against possible invasion.

TOP, EARLY TANK TRIALS IN 1916

CENTRE, TANKS IN SERVICE ON THE WESTERN FRONT, 1917

BOTTOM, THE PRIME MINISTER INSPECTING A CROMWELL TANK, 1944

21

1914, WINSTON CHURCHILL WITH SIR EDWARD GREY, THE FOREIGN MINISTER

FIRST WORLD WAR

Though preparing for what now seemed to him the certainty of war, Churchill was no war-monger. Here he is seen with Sir Edward Grey who, as Foreign Secretary, worked so hard for peace but who with Churchill, was insistent, when Belgium's neutrality was violated in August 1914, that we must stand by our pledge to defend her.

Throughout his years at the Admiralty Churchill had worked to build up a fleet that would be ready when "the day" came. As the war clouds gathered he had organised a test mobilisation and entirely on his own authority had finally despatched the fleet to its action stations. A week later had come war—and his justification. These pictures show (top opposite) The First Battle Cruiser Squadron in 1914; (below opposite) Ships of the First Battle Squadron in line, H.M.S. *Royal Sovereign* (nearest camera), H.M.S. *Resolution* and H.M.S. *Revenge*. The five ships of the *Royal Sovereign* Class, mounting eight 15 inch and fourteen 6 inch guns and with a service speed of 22 knots, were the last battleships to be built for the British Fleet during the First World War. For all his preoccupation with the Fleet Churchill was not a mere "chair-borne" warrior. In the first German drive towards the Channel, Antwerp had been by-passed and at Kitchener's wish the First Lord had hurried there to lend encouragement to the Belgians in a resistance that might save the Channel ports. Taking command Churchill did the job successfully though Antwerp fell and many British lives were lost.

BRITISH TROOPS GOING ASHORE AT THE DARDANELLES

A RECONSTRUCTION OF THE LANDING AT CAPE HELLES, GALLIPOLI, 1915

GALLIPOLI

Gallipoli, name evocative of such heroism and such appalling losses, was the scene of an attempt to neutralise Turkey and link up with Russia by a great diversionary thrust at the enemy's back door. The plan for a naval action to force the Dardanelles was called off by the admiral on the spot after heavy but not crippling losses ; the land forces were not made available in time : the coast was heavily fortified under German supervision during the period of delay, and the final landings could not be successfully maintained. (Below opposite) A diorama representing the Landing on " V " Beach, Cape Helles, 25th April, 1915. (Top opposite) British troops going ashore at the Dardanelles pass H.M.S. *Implacable*.

Removed from the Admiralty, because of his supposed responsibility for the Dardanelles fiasco, Churchill was given the "consolation prize" of Chancellor of the Duchy of Lancaster. But this post with its non-existent duties was not one to appeal to such a man in danger's hour, and 1916 found him on the Western Front, commanding the *6th Royal Scots Fusiliers*, as usual dressed somewhat unconventionally for the part. At first Churchill's arrival was hailed as anything but a blessing by his superior officers. Well acquainted with the spectacular figure he had cut in the past as politician, reporter and naval strategist, they did not realise the capacity for taking pains, the burning enthusiasm, the fearlessness and the genuine gift for leadership upon which the " spectacular figure " was based. They were soon convinced. Those he led needed no convincing.

THE LATER WAR YEARS

When Churchill's battalion and another were amalgamated and no further command came in sight, he realised that his usefulness to the cause could be greater elsewhere and returned to Westminster. At first, as a private member, while Asquith was Prime Minister (top), he was very critical of the Government's handling of the war, but when Lloyd George took over in 1916 peace was patched up. In 1917 Churchill became Minister of Munitions, re-organising, speaking, visiting factories to see the munitions made (below) and visiting France (where the French government gave him his own Chateau) to see them used.

WITH THE PRINCE OF WALES, 1919

Having organised an immense output of munitions for 1919, Churchill found himself put out of a
job by the German collapse in 1918. But he had now acquired a reputation as a " trouble-shooter "
and Lloyd George made him Secretary of State for War and Air (1918-1921). Here he is seen with
the Prince of Wales whom, as King Edward VIII, he was to stand by so tenaciously at the time of
the abdication crisis.

POLITICS IN THE 1920's

The years immediately following the war were to confront Churchill with many problems; all of them demanding immediate solution, many of them, in fact, insoluble. First came the question of demobilisation. An attempt to arrange this on a basis of "priority" in accordance with the needs of Industry had led to a number of ugly riots and mutinies. Churchill at once put in hand a scheme of "first in, first out" which took into account both the soldier's age and the number of times he had been wounded. This saved the day by "massive commonsense". The problems of withdrawing from Archangel the force committed to defending the White Russians against the new regime, of making a settlement between Jews and Arabs in Palestine and of settling the explosive issue of Ireland's independence were all matters that he had to handle either as Secretary for War and Air or as Secretary for the Colonies (1921-1922). Solomon himself might have failed to provide universal satisfaction in these matters. After the fall of the coalition came election defeats at Dundee in 1922 and at Leicester West in 1923 but, undismayed, Churchill still took his relaxation the hard way—on the polo field. When the declining Liberal power appeared to be throwing in its weight with the new force of Labour, Churchill stood as an Independent for the Abbey Division of Westminster where he was defeated by a narrow margin. (Below) An incident during this campaign.

ELECTIONEERING IN THE ABBEY DIVISION OF WESTMINSTER IN 1924

THE GENERAL STRIKE

In November 1924 the Conservative party, ready to support anyone who would oppose the Labour party after its year of power, allowed Churchill to contest the Epping division of Essex, unopposed by them, as a Constitutionalist and he was duly elected. From 1924 to 1929 he held the office of Chancellor of the Exchequer as an accepted Conservative. This period, not one of his most brilliant, was marked by the return of the country to the gold standard (a much disputed move) and by the General Strike which shortly followed it. The fighting Churchill here seen visiting No. 10 Downing Street, " on the eve of battle " joined forces with the journalistic Churchill to produce the " British Gazette "—the only paper to appear during the strike—working it up within a very short time to a circulation of three million. As Editor, Churchill viewed efforts at conciliation with little favour, a fact that was to be remembered against him in later years. It is one of the merits or de-merits of the bulldog, according to whether or not one needs its help, that having got a grip it finds it hard to let go.

29

SPORTS AND PASTIMES

A man of wide interests and bursting with activity, Churchill obviously believes in the old adage that "all work and no play makes Jack a dull boy". Any *less* "dull boy" it would be hard to find. Yet he is by no means the "Jack of all trades" who is "master of none". As orator, historian and journalist he has few rivals to fear; as a painter he commands the respect of the knowledgeable. As Parliamentarian and Statesman he is of course unique—and even as bricklayer the edifices he constructs are acknowledged to be sound. But above all he is a whole man—never content to exalt the mind at the expense of the body or to let a skilful brain rob him of a skilful hand. Contemplation has never been his strong suit (though when reverses have forced him to it, it has borne notable fruit), nor has the pursuit of knowledge for its own sake ever attracted him. But what the brain or the hand can be set to *do*, what the brain or the hand can be made visibly to *bring about*, that—especially, if it involves some element of risk—he will undertake. Fishing or shooting he looks constricted; with a golf club he looks miserable: it is almost impossible to imagine him with a billiard cue.—But given a medium of expression allowing for the sweeping gesture, for dash and bravura, he is at home—and usually "in the forefront of the battle".

LEFT, PHEASANT SHOOTING IN 1910

BELOW, BUILDING A HOUSE AT WESTERHAM, KENT IN 1928, HELPED BY HIS DAUGHTER, SARAH

HUNTING THE WILD BOAR IN FRANCE, 1927

ON A PAINTING HOLIDAY IN MADEIRA, 1950

INTO THE POLITICAL WILDERNESS

The world of figures in which a Chancellor of the Exchequer dwells allows of little "showmanship", provides few excitements and few tangible enemies to be overwhelmed by craft or force—it is not a Churchillian world. Nor was Stanley Baldwin a Churchillian Prime Minister. There were of course good wordy duels with Snowdon in the Commons, and the annual ritual of the budget with its enigmatic smiles and case full of secrets, yet probably it was with some relief that Churchill found himself electioneering again in 1929. But now it seemed that the tide turned against him. Ramsay MacDonald returned to power, and a nation tired of war began to dream that because the world longed for peace it had found it.

Churchill had no such illusions. In 1932 he was already pointing to "the great mass of Russia, with its enormous armies" and warning the country, "If you wish for disarmament, it will be necessary to go to the political and economic causes which lie behind the maintenance of armies and navies". At the same time he spoke most emphatically against acceptance of the concept of "total war" and the bombing of open cities.

CHURCHILL, ACCOMPANIED BY HIS DAUGHTER DIANA, ON HIS WAY TO THE HOUSE OF COMMONS IN 1928 TO PRESENT HIS LAST BUDGET

——In a world of sincere but misguided make-believe Churchill was not acceptable. With the coming of a Coalition government under MacDonald (1931) things were no better, nor were they improved by the return of Baldwin in 1935 or Neville Chamberlain's advent in 1937. Germany was re-arming, yet Churchill's insistent warnings went unregarded. As a private citizen he might entertain Chaplin or come out of hospital smoking a cigar and people took note,—but as a politician he was " dead ".

RIGHT, WITH MR. CHARLES CHAPLIN IN 1931

LEAVING HOSPITAL IN 1932 AFTER AN ATTACK OF PARA-TYPHOID FEVER

KING EDWARD VIII ON BOARD H.M.S. "ECHO" WHILE VISITING THE HOME FLEET

ON BOARD H.M.S. "ENCHANTRESS" AT
THE FLEET REVIEW, 1937

In the long years "in the wilderness" three of Churchill's qualities showed up in all their brightness—his foresight, his perseverance and his loyalty. He warned his country and kept on warning it in the face of apathy, anger and ridicule. He served his king and continued serving him to the last moment without thought of the effect on his own position or career.

Of course the wilderness had its own consolations ; family life with Mrs. Churchill—seen here in a characteristically cheerful pose—and with his children ; time to paint, time to write —we must thank it for *Marlborough*, the four volume life of his great ancestor. Yet, in spite of the cheerfulness, in spite of the hint of "Admiralty" in this picture taken in 1937 aboard H.M.S. *Enchantress*, Churchill was really waiting for the call that came in 1939.

MRS. CHURCHILL AT A TENNIS PARTY

SEPTEMBER, 1939, WINSTON CHURCHILL RETURNS TO THE ADMIRALTY

WAR

Manchuria, Abyssinia, the Rhineland, Axis intervention in Spain, Austria, the Sudetenland, Munich and " peace with honour ", Czechoslovakia ;—the writing had long been on the wall but few had interpreted its fatal message. Now war had come to dismembered Europe and once more, on September 4th, 1939, Churchill was entering the Admiralty as its First Lord.

There was much to be done to safeguard England's seaways. These are the men who—under Churchill's command—saw that it was done—the Board of Admiralty. (Directly under the lamp sits the First Sea Lord and Chief of the Naval Staff, Admiral of the Fleet Sir Dudley Pound.) The arrival of the convoys ; the destruction of the *Graf Spee* in the River Plate ;

the *Cossack's* rescue of the *Altmark* prisoners in a Norwegian fiord—all these speak for the quality of their work. The British expeditionary force too was carried safely to France. Even in these early days of the war it was obvious that Churchill alone amongst the members of Mr. Chamberlain's Cabinet had both the temperament and the knowledge to play " the war game " on the scale and with the temerity that it demanded. In 1938 he had said, " For five years I have talked to the House on these matters—not with very great success. I have watched this famous island descending incontinently, fecklessly, the stairway which leads to a dark gulf." Yet brought back from the wilderness in the hour of need he bore no grudge and was the first to pay tribute to the principles of the leader whose " appeasement " policy he had fought so relentlessly.

THE BOARD OF ADMIRALTY IN SESSION

THE FIRST YEAR OF WAR

In a country woefully unprepared there was much to do, but mercifully there was a lull before the storm, in the shape of the nine month " phoney war ". In this time Churchill " looked to his moat " both at the Admiralty, and on personal visits to England's many miles of coastal defences. He might have said then, as he was to say later, " we have our faults, and our social system has its faults, but we hope that, with God's help, we shall be able to prove for all time, or at any rate, for a long time, that a State or Commonwealth of democracy, possesses amid the sharpest shocks the faculty of survival in a high and honourable and, indeed, in a glorious degree."

February 1940. Here is the Churchill that the world was to come to know so well. Under the guns of the *Exeter* (opposite) he speaks to her crew on their return from the River Plate. The " greyhounds " had been loosed from the " slips " and they had done their work well. He surveys them with a sombre, a humble, a determined pride and stands rock-like before them to render thanks.

INSPECTING DEFENCES OF SOUTHERN COMMAND, 1940

ADDRESSING THE CREW OF H.M.S. " EXETER " ON THEIR RETURN FROM THE SINKING OF THE " GRAF SPEE "
AT THE BATTLE OF THE RIVER PLATE

MR. CHURCHILL'S WAR CABINET IN THE SPRING OF 1941

Mr. Churchill's War Cabinet (as in the Spring of 1941), (back row: left to right) Mr. Arthur Greenwood, *Minister without Portfolio*; Mr. Ernest Bevin, *Minister of Labour*; Lord Beaverbrook, *Minister of Aircraft Production*; Sir Kingsley Wood, *Chancellor of the Exchequer*. (Front row: left to right) Sir John Anderson, *Lord President of the Council*; Mr. Winston Churchill, *Prime Minister*; Mr. Clement Attlee, *Lord Privy Seal*; Mr. Anthony Eden, *Foreign Secretary*.

DUNKIRK

By the will of the country Churchill had become Prime Minister on May 10th, 1940. When the German attack came and France began to crumble, he flew to Paris twice and made his great offer of Union between France and England, but in vain. The trapped British army had to be saved by the " little ships "—and by a miracle of fine weather—from the beaches of Dunkirk between May 28th and 3rd June.

To the rest of the world the fall of France seemed to herald the final triumph of Germany. Yet in England there was neither talk nor thought of surrender. Pillboxes became more numerous ; identity cards were more often scanned—that was all.

OUR FINEST HOUR

Now England stood alone in her " finest hour ". With an army half of whose arms and equipment had had to be left on the beaches of France she awaited invasion, and with a handful of fighter planes, Spitfires (below) and Hurricanes, she challenged—and by the end of September had broken—the power of Germany's Luftwaffe. " Never in the field of human conflict was so much owed by so many to so few." For the rest it was " blood, toil, tears and sweat " that Churchill offered. New forces and weapons had to be prepared, but in the meantime the Churchill spirit fired the country through his broadcasts, and the Commandos —an institution after his own heart—offered a foretaste of better things to the people of subjugated Europe.

Meanwhile London was " taking it ". Never had a city withstood such a prolonged and terrible ordeal. Above St. Paul's the vapour trails turned and twisted (opposite), and by night the sky glowed redly behind the great dome and the Cross. The Anderson shelter became a feature of most back gardens ; the late traveller in the Underground saw ranks of sleepers swathed in overcoats and rugs lining the platforms ; firewatchers paced the rooftops and Wardens herded their often reluctant charges out of sight, if not out of hearing, of the battle. And undismayed Churchill was saying, " even if all the homes of the country be levelled, then we shall still be found standing together to build them up again after the fighting is over."

FIGHTERS OVER ST. PAUL'S

FIRES ROUND ST. PAUL'S

HURRICANES

THE SINKING OF THE " BISMARCK "

THE TURNING POINT, 1941

1941 was the turning point of the war. Britain entered it alone, financially at a low ebb, menaced with starvation by her shipping losses in the Atlantic, successful admittedly in North Africa but only against the weaker of the Axis partners, Italy. But the weapons were being made—Churchill was there to try them ; the convoys, with increasingly active assistance from America were getting through—Churchill was there to thank and encourage their crews. Yet there were many disasters to be faced. Greece was supported in her struggle and lost. Crete was lost. In North Africa Rommel pushed back our army, depleted by these campaigns, to the borders of Egypt. Yet Churchill's attitude remained what it had been in 1940 to his commanders in the field ;—they must be trusted and supported. " I have endeavoured always to say that those who launch themselves against the enemy in any action, with vigour and violence will, whatever the upshot, receive the support of His Majesty's Government." In Parliament there was strong criticism of the government, especially after the sinking of the *Hood*, a graceful but old and all too vulnerable battle-cruiser in which armour had been sacrificed to speed. Churchill rode the flood, not as a dictator— though he could be dictatorial—but in the clear knowledge that he remained the man for the job. In his humility, however, there was always likely to be steel. " I do not at all resent criticism, even when, for the sake of emphasis, it for a time parts company with reality."—The *Bismarck* was sunk (above) : the *Hood* was avenged.

MAY, 1941

Mr. Churchill contemplates the ruins of the House of Commons, bombed in May 1941. " We must have spirits so constant that we can derive from misfortune added strength. . . . We cannot tell how long the road will be. We only know that it will be stony, painful and uphill, and that we shall march along it to the end."

IN THE STREETS OF
BIRMINGHAM

" To leave the offices in Whitehall with their ceaseless hum of activity and stress, and to go out to the front, by which I mean the streets and wharves of London or Liverpool, Manchester, Cardiff, Swansea or Bristol, is like going out of a hothouse on to the bridge of a fighting ship. It is a tonic which I should recommend."—It was a tonic Churchill often took himself. But his work had still to be done, even if—as here—it was done on the train between two engagements. And good news was coming to the " fighting ship ", for, as Hitler turned on Russia in the summer, its people found themselves with a new and powerful ally.

AT WORK DURING A
TRAIN JOURNEY

PRESIDENT ROOSEVELT MEETS THE PRIME MINISTER, 1941

THE PRIME MINISTER AND THE PRESIDENT ON BOARD U.S.S. " AUGUSTA "

"BUT WESTWARD, LOOK, THE LAND IS BRIGHT"

As 1941 passed by, Churchill could fairly quote Clough's line "but westward, look, the land is bright." Under President Roosevelt, the United States was gradually becoming more and more openly implicated in the struggle. "Lease lend" had brought England much needed escort vessels. Wendell Wilkie had come to England as Roosevelt's personal representative to meet Churchill. Finally Premier and President had met in the middle of the Atlantic, aboard the U.S. Cruiser *Augusta*, and had drawn up a joint statement of faith for the future—*The Atlantic Charter*. This union, already so strong, was to be cemented in the last month of the year by disaster. America was to suffer at Pearl Harbour her most crippling naval loss of all time with the undeclared entry of Japan into the war, and Britain was to see her Far Eastern Empire begin to crumble under the assault of the same enemy after the loss of the *Repulse* and the *Prince of Wales*. —Yet at last America was in the war and that fact outweighed all others. Churchill did not leave the Americans to imagine the welcome he owed them but posted off again across the Atlantic to address the Senate. "Now that we are together, now that we are linked in a righteous comradeship of arms . . . a new scene opens upon which a steady light will glow and brighten."

JANUARY, 1942, MR. CHURCHILL ADDRESSING A JOINT SESSION OF THE U.S. CONGRESS

THE WESTERN DESERT

The pictures on this and the opposite page show Churchill on a visit to the Eighth Army in the Western desert during August, 1942. (Left) with General Freyberg, Commander of the 2nd New Zealand Division and (below) with General Wavell who had borne the brunt as Commander in this theatre during the early years but had been succeeded by General Auchinleck, who was now to give way to General Alexander. 1942 had begun disastrously with the loss of Malaya and Singapore to the Japanese and in the desert things had gone little better. But now with General Montgomery in command of the Eighth Army the tide turned. His great victory against Rommel at El Alamein was the result, partly of his own brilliance, partly of the planned build-up of supplies pushed ahead with by Churchill during the dark days of 1941. From now on Montgomery was to drive Rommel westwards until, with the aid of the Americans, Africa was eventually cleared of Axis troops by May 1943. From there the first attack was to be launched on Europe as General Alexander swept through Sicily in July 1943 and on to Italy in September. Meanwhile Russia after a " scorched earth " retreat to Stalingrad had stopped the German advance and was taking terrible toll of the invader——

WITH GENERAL FREYBERG

IN CAIRO WITH GENERAL SIR ARCHIBALD WAVELL AND LT.-COL. SIR SIKANDER HYAT KHAN

SHAKING HANDS WITH A SERGEANT OF AN ARMOURED BRIGADE

AT A DESERT CEMETERY

INSPECTING COMMANDOS

THREE-POWER CONFERENCE IN N. AFRICA. CHURCHILL, ROOSEVELT, CHIANG KAI-SHEK AND MADAME CHIANG

PLANNING FOR VICTORY

——But back in England all thoughts were directed to the "Second Front" for which Russia was clamouring and which now began to seem, for the first time, a practical possibility. Behind all the preparations were the drive and energy of the Prime Minister as he bombarded the service ministries with memoranda, worked through a ceaseless round of visits to units (such as the commandos opposite) pressed the necessary measures through Parliament and by his broadcasts carried the nation forward from the spirit of "we can take it" to the idea of "the liberation of Europe". In operation "Overlord" the 21*st Army Group* under General Montgomery was to take the lead, but even this immense undertaking was for Churchill only one facet of a world-wide situation for which he had to plan. The links with a Russia who demanded much—and was prepared to give little—in co-operation, had to be cemented by a further meeting at Teheran between Roosevelt, Stalin and Churchill. Plans had to be laid for the re-conquest of the Far East in co-operation with the U.S.A. and China. The bottom picture on the opposite page shows the President and the Prime Minister with General and Madame Chiang-Kai-Shek, and in the back row can be seen (right) Major-General Carton de Wiart, (second from right) Admiral Lord Louis Mountbatten, Supreme Allied Commander and (fourth from left) Lieutenant-General Stilwell, Commanding General U.S. Forces in China.

1943, STALIN, ROOSEVELT AND CHURCHILL AT THE TEHERAN CONFERENCE

A MULBERRY PIERHEAD OFF ARROMANCHES

MULBERRY PIERHEADS IN LINE

MULBERRY

When the invasion came on June 6th, 1944 it turned out to be quite unlike any operation staged before. In the past any landing made in strength against an enemy coast had always necessitated the capture of a port. Even with the amazing advances made by the Americans in the use of amphibious landing craft for getting men, vehicles and tanks ashore, no adequate build-up of supplies could have been maintained without a port had it not been for the *Mulberries*. In these movable harbours, units like that pictured (opposite above) could be fixed in place off the coast to act as floating piers, rising and falling with the tide. Protected by old merchant ships and caissons sunk further out to form a breakwater and connected to the shore by pontoon bridges, they were capable of handling very heavy traffic. For this invention, which left the allied commanders free to choose their landing place where it would cause the most surprise and meet the least opposition, we have, at least in part, to thank Mr. Churchill,— for the idea evolved from a memorandum of his, produced several years earlier.

The rest of the plans for the invasion had been made with the same mixture of boldness, ingenuity and attention to detail. Reconnaissance raids, and a mass of holiday snapshots of the French coast, collected from the British public as the result of an appeal, had given an idea of the problem to be faced. Frogmen were trained for dealing with under-water obstacles. A process was evolved for " waterproofing " vehicles so that they could wade ashore. " *Pluto* " the pipeline that was to carry petrol under the Channel had been constructed.

AMBULANCES USING A MULBERRY PIER

THE INVASION

On *D. Day* General Eisenhower, Supreme Commander Allied Powers in Europe had said in his order of the day, "The eyes of the world are upon you. The hopes and prayers of liberty-loving people everywhere march with you." No-one could have been more eager to carry his prayers with the invading army in person than Churchill, but his plea was understandably and wisely over-ruled. Yet only six days later he crosses the Channel and soon after is getting his first view of the new battlefields and talking in Caen to troops who took part in the initial assault. After a pause to consolidate, the allied armies are off across Europe towards a Germany that through the years has lost command of the air and has been bombed to the point where her industries are failing her——

——But Hitler has still two unpleasant surprises in reserve for England,—surprises that owing to the same cause have had to wait overlong to be effective. The flying bomb and the rocket are loosed on London to do their wanton damage, but as the allied forces sweep northwards and their launching sites are captured the menace is overcome.

MR. CHURCHILL, WITH ADMIRAL VIAN AND F.M. SIR ALAN BROOKE, ON HIS WAY TO THE NORMANDY BEACHES

WITH THE TROOPS IN NORMANDY

A FLYING BOMB TAKES OFF

A V.I. INCIDENT, JULY, 1944

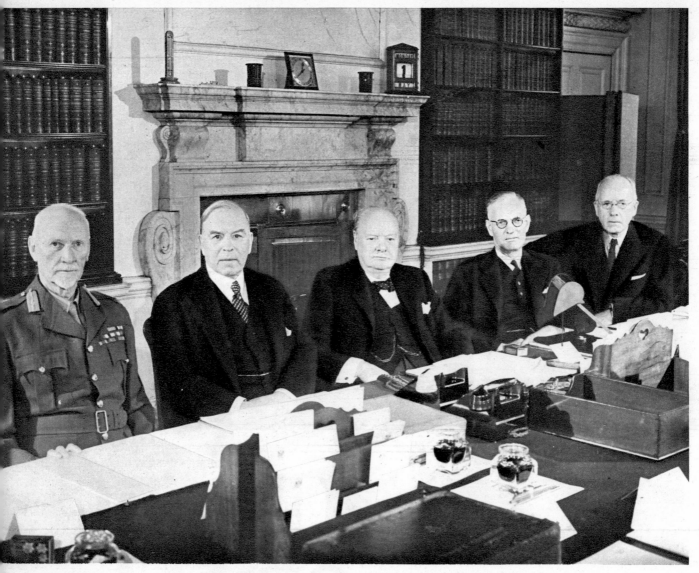

MR. CHURCHILL WITH THE COMMONWEALTH PRIME MINISTERS

For all Churchill's foreign contacts in matters of strategy and post-war planning, it is never absent from his mind that he is working not only for a country and for an alliance of friendly nations but also for the linked British Commonwealth and Empire. Here he is seen in more peaceful surroundings at a conference of Commonwealth Premiers held shortly before D. Day. With him are (left to right) General Smuts, *South Africa* ; Mr. Mackenzie King, *Canada* ; Mr. J. Curtin, *Australia* ; and Mr. Peter Fraser, *New Zealand*.

Peace in Europe is now in sight. The invading armies are over the Rhine, after the Germans' last desperate throw, the Ardennes offensive. Churchill is there to see, to cross the Rhine also and to talk with Eisenhower the Commander with whom his relations have always been so friendly and so successful. But for long months now Churchill's main preoccupation has been the

world that must be rebuilt after the war. There is still Japan to be dealt with but, once the allies can concentrate their full strength against her, victory is only a matter of time. But what will Russia do ? Perhaps he regrets that cherished plan of his—the invasion through Eastern Europe. Now Russia has swallowed Eastern Europe. Roosevelt trusts her ; Churchill does not. For some time it has been evident that Stalin has been working on that fear of " British Imperialism ", native to every American, in his dealings with Roosevelt. For Churchill, a thorough European as well as a world statesman, the old idea of the " Balance of Power " still seems to be vital unless and until something better can be worked out. For many hundreds of years England has believed that no continental power must be allowed to grow to a strength that will endanger its neighbours. The policy has not always worked but it appears that—as the dentist says—" things would have been much worse without it."

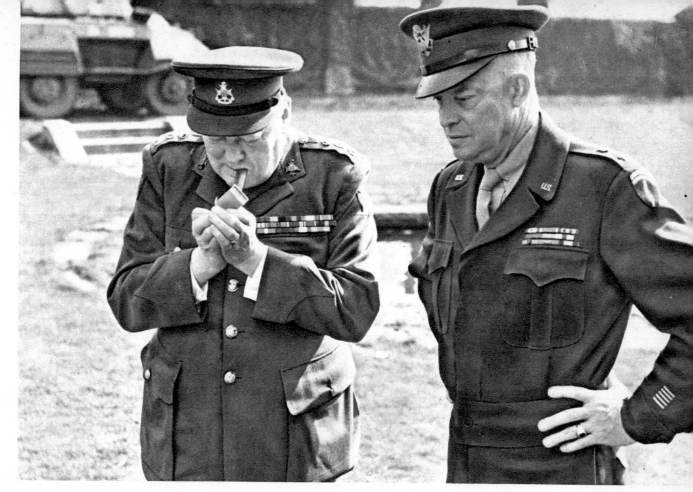

WITH THE SUPREME COMMANDER, GENERAL EISENHOWER

ACROSS THE RHINE

VICTORY

Yet when the day of victory comes, forebodings are temporarily forgotten in rejoicing. Field Marshal Montgomery accepts the surrender of Germany watched by (left to right) Rear Admiral Wagner and General Admiral Von Friedeburg. Later on May 8th 1945, V.E. Day, Churchill speaks to the world. " Hostilities will end officially at one minute after midnight tonight, but in the interests of saving lives the ' Cease Fire ' began yesterday to be sounded all along the front. . . . Advance, Britannia. Long live the cause of freedom. God Save the King."

Before the day is over he is at Buckingham Palace, sharing with the Royal Family the applause of the crowds. Behind these peaceful scenes Europe is witnessing the drawing together of the two great allied armies on a line which, though at the time only a convenient meeting place, is to become that Iron Curtain which is for years to divide the world into two armed camps. Russia now hurries into the war against Japan, eager for expansion towards the east and already infiltrating into the counsels of Communist China.

F.M. MONTGOMERY RECEIVES THE GERMAN SURRENDER

THE KING WITH HIS WAR CABINET, INCLUDING MR. CHURCHILL, MR. ATTLEE AND MR. BEVIN

V.E. DAY AT BUCKINGHAM PALACE

MR. CHURCHILL'S V.E. DAY BROADCAST

BRITISH VICTORY PARADE IN BERLIN, JULY, 1945

MR. CHURCHILL, GENERALISSIMO STALIN, AND PRESIDENT TRUMAN MEET IN BERLIN, JULY, 1945

Mr. Churchill goes to Berlin for the Victory Parade in July 1945. 10,000 men representing Britain's Fighting Services march past him in the Charlottenburger Chaussee for 40 minutes. Mr. Churchill is seen (opposite) inspecting the tanks of the *Desert Rats* in company with Field Marshal Sir Bernard Montgomery and Field Marshal Sir Alan Brooke. Two days later the three Chiefs of State meet. Roosevelt, that generous, courageous, perhaps over-optimistic man, is dead and has been succeeded by President Truman. The atmosphere seems cordial. But half way around the world the " cloud no bigger than a man's hand " is waiting to " mushroom " over Hiroshima and Nagasaki. That, more than the friendly smiles, is what now preserves peace between the western and eastern allies.

KING GEORGE VI PRESENTS THE FREEDOM OF THE SHIPWRIGHTS COMPANY TO MR. CHURCHILL, AT THE
MANSION HOUSE, 1945

" The tumult and the shouting dies ; the Captains and the Kings depart." Scarcely was victory
in Europe won than the country found itself in the throes of an election and Churchill, though
retaining his own seat, saw his party decisively beaten at the polls. Later, near the time of his
resignation, he was to make a clear statement of his creed as a politician and, perhaps this is the
place for it—for some failures are more noble than successes. " The first duty of an M.P. is to do
what in his faithful and disinterested judgment he believes is right and necessary for the honour
and safety of our beloved country. The second duty is to his constituents, of whom he is the
representative but not the delegate. It is only in the third place that a man's duty to the party
organisation or programme takes rank. All those three should be observed but there is no doubt
of the order in which they stand in any healthy manifestation of democracy."—For a time the
" country's leader " was gone but the " man whom the King delighteth to honour " remained.

MR. ATTLEE AND MR. CHURCHILL LEAVING WESTMINSTER ABBEY AFTER ATTENDING A MEMORIAL SERVICE
FOR F.M. LORD GORT, V.C., APRIL, 1946

65

1947, MR. CHURCHILL, AS HONORARY AIR COMMODORE OF 615 SQUADRON, REVISITS BIGGIN HILL

AT BIGGIN HILL—CHURCHILL THE WAR LEADER REMEMBERS 1940 AND " THE FEW "

At Fulton in 1946 Churchill the World Statesman warns " Beware, I say ; time may be short. . . . It is my duty to place before you certain facts about the present position in Europe . . . an iron curtain has descended across the Continent . . . in a great number of countries far from the Russian frontiers and throughout the world, Communist fifth columns are established."

As Leader of the Opposition, however, Churchill has his moments of pleasure. As he was once heard to say, " the spectacle of a number of middle-aged gentlemen who are my political opponents being in a state of uproar and fury is really quite exhilarating to me ". Nevertheless it is primarily the *man* who appeals to the public eye during this period.

WITH MRS. CHURCHILL ON HIS 74TH BIRTHDAY, NOVEMBER 30, 1948

If after the war the country had turned against Mr. Churchill as the leader of a political party, England and the world still acknowledged thankfully his pre-eminence as wartime leader, statesman and " personality ".   Honours were showered on him, including the Grotius medal for services in the cause of peace and an honorary degree from Cambridge University.   In any case the Labour tide was ebbing.   Their majority at the 1950 election was down to five seats.

MR. CHURCHILL RECEIVES AN HONORARY DEGREE AT CAMBRIDGE

THE CROWD CHEERS A VICTORY FOR MR. CHURCHILL'S "COLONIST II" AT WINDSOR, 1949

CHEERS AGAIN AS MR. CHURCHILL GOES TO VOTE IN THE 1951 GENERAL ELECTION

THE FAMOUS V-SIGN

Victory on the race-course gives way to victory at the polls in 1951 and Mr. Churchill is once again Prime Minister. "V for Victory" implies no "devil take the hindmost" reversal of what has been good in the Welfare State but a policy of expansion at home and "containment" abroad.

AT HARROW SCHOOL, 1951

WITH SIR ABDUL RAHMAN EL-MAHDI AT DOWNING STREET

RELAXATION

In the intervals of working for a closer relationship between France and Germany and smoothing out the rough places of Anglo-American co-operation ; between efforts to come to grips with the Russian problem by arranging top-level talks ; between troubles about the Canal Zone, troubles soon to arise in Malaya and Kenya and the ever-present knowledge of war raging in Korea, the Prime Minister could enjoy few moments of real relaxation. But here he is seen in two of them (opposite above) at his old school, Harrow, and (opposite below) with Sayed Sir Abdul Rahman el-Mahdi, leader of a Sudanese delegation in London and son of his opponent at Omdurman. Mr. Churchill's home, when he has not been officially in residence at No. 10 Downing Street, has for many years been at Chartwell Manor, Westerham. Here he has written many of his books, composed many of his speeches, entertained, relaxed, " made improvements " (notably with bricks and mortar) and gathered his family around him.

CHARTWELL MANOR

MR. AND MRS. CHURCHILL AT CHARTWELL ON MR. CHURCHILL'S 77TH BIRTHDAY

THE CHURCHILL FAMILY

Seeing politicians always on the hustings or against the background of " the best club in the world "—as the Mother of Parliaments has been called—it is easy to forget that each of them has behind his public self his own private life, his *home* life. Father of a son and four daughters (one of whom died in infancy), Mr. Churchill has been followed in his parliamentary career not only by his son, Randolph, but by two of his sons-in-law, Mr. Duncan Sandys (married to Diana) and Captain Christopher Soames (married to Mary). His other daughter, Sarah, is of course the well-known actress, while a niece, Clarissa, is married to Sir Anthony Eden.

SARAH CHURCHILL, THE ACTRESS

MRS. SOAMES, NÉE MARY CHURCHILL

WINSTON CHURCHILL AND HIS GRANDCHILDREN, 1951

AT THE CHRISTENING OF CHARLOTTE SOAMES, NOVEMBER, 1954

MR. CHURCHILL WITH HIS GRANDSON, NICHOLAS SOAMES, IN 1952

(Opposite above) " Three generations ". (Left to right) Mr. Duncan Sandys ; Mrs. Duncan Sandys (formerly Diana Churchill) ; Julian Sandys ; Emma Soames (on Mr. Churchill's knee) ; Nicholas Soames ; Winston (Randolph Churchill's son) ; Arabella (young Winston's sister), and Mr. Randolph Churchill. (Opposite below) A family occasion. In the foreground of the group are the three Soames children, Nicholas, Emma, and—youngest—Jeremy. On the right stands Captain Soames and next him his wife holds their baby, Charlotte Clementine. On the left is Mr. Fitzroy Maclean, one of the baby's godfathers and beside him stands Mrs. Duncan Sandys. On this page two great men are seen in a relaxed mood. Mr. Churchill at the christening of Jeremy Soames, in August, 1952, walks hand in hand with his four-year-old grandson, Nicholas Soames, followed by Field Marshal Viscount Montgomery of Alamein, the new baby's godfather.

SIR WINSTON CHURCHILL LEAVING ST. GEORGE'S CHAPEL, WINDSOR AFTER HIS INSTALLATION

On April 24th, 1953 the Queen confers upon the Right Hon. Winston Churchill, M.P. the honour of Knighthood and invests him with the Insignia of a Knight Companion of the Most Noble Order of the Garter. Later on June 14th, 1954 Sir Winston Churchill is formally installed into the Order in a ceremony at St. George's Chapel, Windsor. During 1953, in Russia, Premier Stalin died, and for a time it seemed possible that under his successor, Mr. Malenkov, an era of greater co-operation might begin. However, with Malenkov's fall next year, the old uncertainties returned.

OUTSIDE ST. GEORGE'S CHAPEL, AMONG THE HERALDS

SIR WINSTON AND LADY CHURCHILL ON THEIR WAY TO WESTMINSTER ABBEY

In May and June of 1953 two great events—happy auguries for England's future—took place within a few days of each other. Sir John Hunt's expedition conquered Everest and England's young and gracious Queen was Crowned at Westminster Abbey. This latter ceremony impressed the world to a totally unexpected degree, not so much by its magnificence as by the quiet dignity and obvious self-dedication of its central figure. Though the weather on Coronation Day was poor and rain fell

CORONATION

THE QUEEN PASSES IN PROCESSION DOWN THE NAVE OF THE ABBEY

as the great processions wound their way through London, the fervour of the crowds was unabated and, apart from the Royal Family, their applause rose louder for no-one than for the Prime Minister. Now the crowds were seeing him among the symbols of history. But a few years before they had, under his leadership, been *making* history.

It has been variously written of Churchill that his oratory depends entirely on his magnificent powers as a writer and that his writing is merely the transcription of brilliant oratory. Whatever be the correct answer the fact remains that, whether in impromptu exchanges in the House, on the platform or at the microphone, he has an unequalled power to spur, delight, elevate or castigate his audience. The Churchillian touch is as characteristic as the Nelson touch—and probably as indefinable.

ABOVE, AT COUNTY HALL, LONDON IN THE DARK DAYS OF 1941

OPPOSITE, AT THE CONSERVATIVE PARTY CONFERENCE, 1947

BELOW, AT A UNITED EUROPE MEETING, 1950

SIR WINSTON CHURCHILL LEAVES FOR WASHINGTON, 1954

AN 80TH BIRTHDAY PRESENTATION BY SIR WINSTON'S CONSTITUENTS AT WOODFORD, ESSEX

In 1954 the great problems confronting the Western Alliance were whether or not Western Germany should be re-armed, the future of Formosa and the progress of Communism in the various colonial territories in South East Asia. Abroad, England had a problem of her own in Kenya with the emergence of Mau Mau terrorism. Churchill, determined that the link with America shall be maintained undamaged by differences of viewpoint, sets off, in June, for Washington. 1954 also brings his eightieth birthday.

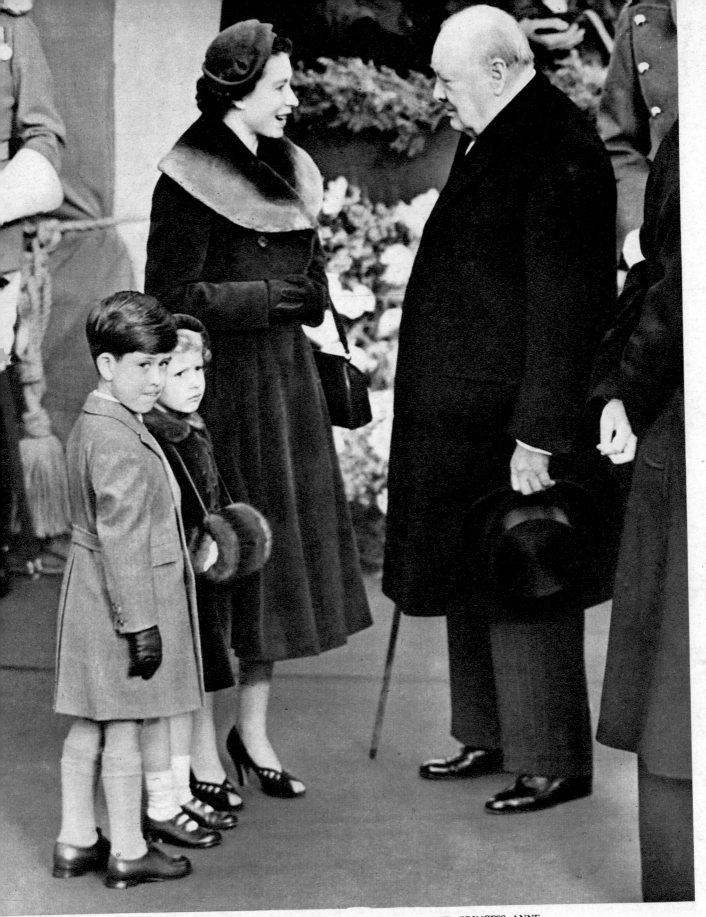

WITH HER MAJESTY THE QUEEN, PRINCE CHARLES AND PRINCESS ANNE

SIR WINSTON RECEIVES AN 80TH BIRTHDAY GIFT FROM THE BRITISH LEGION

The arrival of Sir Winston's eightieth birthday on November 30th, 1954 brought forth tributes and gifts from all over the world. A birthday fund, whose original impetus came not from any official body but from a few private citizens, was soon receiving contributions on a scale never before known in such a case. Gifts of flowers, food, money, wine, cigars, and personal souvenirs connected with incidents in his past life, poured in to No. 10 Downing Street. One tribute, moving on account of its source as well as its nature, was the leather-bound illuminated address given by the British Legion. The President of the Legion, Sir Ian Fraser, M.P., is seated beside Mr. Churchill in the photograph.

(Opposite) A pleasant, informal study of Sir Winston with the Queen and the royal children as they wait for the return of the Queen Mother on her return from her most successful and warmly received visit to Canada and America in the autumn of 1954.

SIR WINSTON AND LADY CHURCHILL IN WESTMINSTER HALL FOR AN 80TH BIRTHDAY PRESENTATION BY
LORDS AND COMMONS

Parliament's own celebration of the eightieth birthday of one of its most remarkable members took the form of two presentations in Westminster Hall. Mr. Attlee, the Leader of the Opposition, gave Sir Winston, on behalf of both the Lords and the Commons a portrait painted by Mr. Graham Sutherland, while Mr. D. R. Grenfell handed him a beautifully illuminated address signed by almost all those M.P.'s who have served with him.

Opinions regarding the presentation portrait varied from the lyrical to the vituperative. The Prime Minister's own ambiguous comment, " a remarkable example of modern Art " left the scales swinging uneasily.

THE PRESENTATION CEREMONY IN WESTMINSTER HALL, NOVEMBER 30, 1954

THE QUEEN WITH HER PRIME MINISTERS, FEBRUARY, 1955

February 1955. Churchill with the Queen and the Dominion Prime Ministers. (Left to right) Sir Godfrey Huggins, *Central Africa Federation* ; Mr. Mohammed Ali, *Pakistan* ; Mr. Robert Menzies, *Australia* ; Mr. Charles Swart (representing *South Africa's* Prime Minister) : Mr. Sidney Holland, *New Zealand* ; Mr. Louis St. Laurent, *Canada* ; Pandit Jawaharlal Nehru, *India* ; Sir John Kotelawala, *Ceylon.*

(Opposite) For the last time as her Prime Minister, Sir Winston welcomes the Queen and the Duke of Edinburgh to No. 10 Downing Street on the evening of April 4th, 1955. About to lay down office, he can look back with pride to his Government's record, at home, in building new houses and encouraging the expansion of Industry and, abroad, in working for peace and harmony among the nations.

On April 5th, 1955 the pilot who weathered the storm steps down from the bridge and, true to form at the last, catches everyone napping. London's newspaper presses are at a halt—strikebound— but for him the usual laudatory columns in their pages could do little. He has his secure place in the hearts and memories of countless millions the world over. For them the simple announcement of his resignation is all that is needed. They can supply their own grateful valediction.

SIR WINSTON AND LADY CHURCHILL WELCOME THE QUEEN AT NO. 10 DOWNING STREET

FAREWELL TO DOWNING STREET, APRIL 5, 1955

Another phase of Sir Winston's career comes to a close. Like the Phoenix, however, he has the habit of rising from the ashes of one self to the glories of another, and he is still in many ways— as when he was first given the label over fifty years ago—"the youngest man in Europe". Our book ends with Sir Winston, once more a back-bencher, but most emphatically not a back number, perpetuated in bronze and ready to gaze out across the Guildhall for many centuries to come. What

OSCAR NEMON'S BRONZE STATUE OF SIR WINSTON IN LONDON'S GUILDHALL

the future will think of him we cannot know, but while it has his dogged determination visibly present before it and the chronicles of his time to consult we may be sure he will neither be ignored nor forgotten. That there will be a future for humanity, as well as for his statue, Sir Winston himself is convinced. Of the statue he has said, "a very good likeness"; of the world's future, "I do not believe that humanity is going to destroy itself".

Made and Printed in Great Britain by L.T.A. Robinson Limited, London, S.W.9